BEATLES CLASSICS

Midi Keyboard Library

Exclusive Distributors:

Music Sales Limited
8/9 Frith Street,
London W1V 5TZ, England.

Music Sales Pty Limited
120 Rothschild Avenue,
Rosebery, NSW 2018,
Australia.

Order No.NO90496
ISBN 0-7119-3127-5
This book © Copyright 1992 & 1994 by Wise Publications

Book & pack design by 4i Limited
Arrangements by Rick Cardinali
Music processed by Angel Graphics

Printed in the United Kingdom by
Caligraving Limited, Thetford, Norfolk.

Photographs courtesy of:
London Features International

Your Guarantee of Quality

As publishers, we strive to produce every book to the highest commercial standards.
The music has been freshly engraved and this book has been carefully designed to minimise awkward
page turns and to make playing from it a real pleasure. Throughout, the printing and binding have
been planned to ensure a sturdy, attractive publication which should give years of enjoyment. If your
copy fails to meet our high standards, please inform us and we will gladly replace it.

Music Sales' complete catalogue describes thousands of titles and is available in full colour sections
by subject, direct from Music Sales Limited. Please state your areas of interest and send a
cheque/postal order for £1.50 for postage to: Music Sales Limited, Newmarket Road,
Bury St. Edmunds, Suffolk IP33 3YB.

Playing Hints

Included with this book you will find a brand new kind of music data disk. On this 3.5" disk are digitally recorded Standard MIDI Files (SMF). These files or songs can be played on any dedicated or computer based Standard MIDI File player which conforms to the General MIDI system (GM).

The files contain a professionally recorded accompaniment and melody for each song which you can either listen to or play along with. To play the melody of each song (and improvise using the 'Solo Notes'), you must mute the MIDI Channel (track) where this data is recorded. According to the instructions for your particular player, mute MIDI Channel 4, or the track where this channel is located.

Now play the melody along with the accompaniment. To improvise easily with the accompaniment see 'Solo Notes' in the following playing hints.

The songs in this book have been specially arranged to make it easy for you to play along with them. The accompaniment section in some keyboards does not recognise some of the special (complex) chords in each song. These chords are printed in a grey tone and can be ignored if either your keyboard doesn't have the capability to play them or if you yourself have not learned these. Of course, when the time comes that you can play all special chords, a superior harmony sound will be heard.

Solo Notes

Wherever you see the Solo Notes logo you can improvise very easily your own instant melody. In this case the logo shown above has dots on the C, D, E, G and A keys. Each of these notes can be played, one at a time, in any order along with the backing track (Music Minus One). Solo Notes may be played through any measure (bar) over which the 'Grey Line' is shown. This varies in length from song to song.

Improvising Hints

1. Start by positioning your fingers over the notes indicated with the dots. Now start playing one of the designated Solo Notes somewhere in the middle of these keys in the melody (upper) section of your keyboard, in any octave.
2. Decide whether your Instant Melody will go up or down (left or right on the keyboard).
3. Then most of the time play the Solo Note nearest to the one you are currently playing (up or down). Occasionally take a 'longer step' by missing out one or two Solo Note keys. This will add further realism to your 'instant melody' and give further enjoyment to your playing.
4. Play along with the beat (or natural tapping rhythm) of the track.
5. You may find that some notes sound better with the accompaniment than others at different times. If you play a note that does not sound good against the accompaniment, simply move to the nearest Solo Note up or down.

Disk Contents

1.	Yesterday	5.	Lady Madonna
2.	With A Little Help From My Friends	6.	Hey Jude
3.	Eleanor Rigby	7.	Penny Lane
4.	Michelle	8.	Let It Be

Refer to the Owner's Manual of your Standard MIDI File player for the procedure of loading and playing the above files.

Conseils D'Utilisation

Inclus dans ce livre, vous trouverez une toute nouvelle sorte de disquettes de données musicales. Sur cette disquette de 3.5" des Fichiers au Standard MIDI (SMF) sont enregistrés numériquement. Ces fichiers ou morceaux peuvent être joués sur tous les lecteurs de fichiers au Standard MIDI qui sont conformes au système General MIDI (GM).

Les fichiers comprennent un accompagnement et une mélodie enregistrés professionnellement pour chaque morceau que vous pouvez simplement écouter ou bien jouer en même temps. Pour jouer la mélodie de chaque morceau (et improviser en jouant les "Notes Solo"), vous devez couper le canal MIDI (piste) où ces données sont enregistrées. D'après les instructions de votre lecteur MIDI File, couper le canal MIDI 4, ou la piste où ce canal est situé.

Maintenant, vous pouvez jouer avec l'accompagnement. Il est très facile d'improviser avec l'accompagnement en lisant la partie intitulée "Notes Solo" décrite ci-dessous dans les conseils d'utilisation.

Les morceaux de ce livre ont étés organisés spécialement pour qu'il soit facile de jouer en même temps.
La section accompagnement de certains claviers peut ne pas reconnaître quelques-uns des accords complexes dans les morceaux. Ces accords sont enregistrés de telle façon qu'ils peuvent être ignorés si votre clavier n'a pas les capacités de les jouer ou si vous-même ne les avez pas encore appris. Bien sûr, lorsque vous serez capable de jouer tous ces accords spéciaux, l'harmonie sera bien supérieure.

Notes Solo

Lorsque vous voyez le logo "Notes Solo", vous pouvez improviser immédiatement et très aisément votre propre mélodie.
Dans ce cas, le logo, décrit ci-dessus montre des points sur les touches do, ré, mi, sol et la. Chacune de ces notes peut être jouée, une par une, dans n'importe quel ordre en même temps que la piste d'accompagnement (musique moins 1 piste). Les notes solo peuvent être jouées pendant toutes les mesures (barre) sur lesquelles la 'ligne grise' est présente. Ceci varie en terme de durée selon le morceau.

Conseils D'improvisation

1. Commencez par positionner vos doigts sur les notes indiquées par les points. Maintenant commencez à jouer une de ces notes solo dans la partie pour la mélodie (droite) de votre clavier.
2. Décidez alors si la direction de votre 'mélodie instantanée' montera ou descendra (vers la droite ou la gauche du clavier).
3. Alors, essayez de jouer la note solo suivante, soit directement à droite ou à gauche de celle que vous jouez maintenant. De temps en temps, effectuez un 'plus grand écart' en oubliant une ou deux notes solo. Ceci ajoutera un peu plus de réalisme a votre 'mélodie instantanée' et vous donnera encore plus de plaisir.
4. Jouez en suivant le tempo (ou le rythme naturel) du morceau.
5. Vous trouverez des notes plus appropriées que d'autres à l'accompagnement lors de différentes performances. Si vous jouez une note qui ne sonne pas très bien avec l'accompagnement, allez simplement sur la prochaine note solo sur la droite ou sur la gauche.
La piste supplémentaire 'Jam' incluse sur la disquette a été spécialement composée pour vous permettre de créer votre propre mélodie en jouant n'importe laquelle des touches noires, une par une, dans n'importe quel ordre, en même temps que l'accompagnement.
Si vous voulez écouter les sortes de mélodies qui peuvent être crée en utilisant les touches noires, chargez et jouez la piste 'Demo Jam' pour des exemples d'improvisation.

Contenu De La Disquette

1.	Yesterday	5.	Lady Madonna
2.	With A Little Help From My Friends	6.	Hey Jude
3.	Eleanor Rigby	7.	Penny Lane
4.	Michelle	8.	Let It Be

Référrez vous au mode d'emploi de votre lecteur de Fichiers au Standard MIDI pour la procédure de chargement et de lecture des fichiers ci-dessus.

Trucos Para Tocar

Incluído con este libro, usted encontrará un nuevo tipo de disco con información musical. En este disco de 3.5" hay Standard MIDI Files (SMF) grabados digitalmente. Estos archivos o canciones pueden reproducirse en cualquier reproductor de Standard MIDI Files, ya sea dedicado o basado en ordenador, que sea conforme con el sistema General MIDI (GM).

Cada una de las canciones de estos archivos contiene un acompañamiento grabado digitalmente junto con una melodía que usted puede tocar o simplemente escuchar. Para tocar la melodía de cada canción (o improvisar utilizando las 'Notas de Solo'), deberá enmudecer el Canal MIDI (pista) donde está grabada esta información. Siguiendo las instrucciones de su reproductor de MIDI files en particular, enmudezca el Canal MIDI 4, o la pista en la que esté este Canal.

Ahora toque la melodía junto con el acompañamiento. Es fácil improvisar con el acompañamiento siguiendo las 'Notas de Solo' comentadas más abajo en los Trucos para tocar.

Las canciones de este libro se han arreglado especialmente para que a usted le resulte fácil tocarlas. La sección de acompañamiento de ciertos teclados puede que no reproduzca algunos de los acordes especiales (complejos) de cada canción. Estos acordes están impresos en gris y pueden ignorarse en el caso de que su teclado no pueda tocarlos o si usted aún no los ha aprendido. Por supuesto, en cuanto usted pueda tocar todos los acordes especiales, obtendrá unas armonías más ricas.

Notas De Solo

Allí donde vea el logo "Solo Notes", podrá improvisar muy facilmente su propia melodía instantánea. En ese caso, el logo mostrado arriba tiene puntos en las teclas Do, Re, Mi, Sol y La. Cada una de estas notas puede tocarse, en cualquier orden, junto con la pista de acompañamiento (Music Minus One). Las Notas de Solo pueden tocarse en cualquier compás sobre el que se muestre la 'línea gris'. Su longitud varía de una canción a otra.

Trucos Para Improvisar

1. Empiece por poner los dedos sobre las notas indicadas con los puntos. De entre estas Notas de Solo, empiece por tocar una de las de en medio en la sección de melodía (upper) de su teclado, en cualquier octava.
2. Decida si su 'Melodía Instantánea' subirá o bajará (hacia la derecha o izquierda del teclado).
3. A continuación toque la siguiente Nota de Solo, ya sea hacia arriba o hacia abajo. De vez en cuando haga un 'paso más largo' saltándose una o dos teclas de las Notas de Solo. Esto añadirá más realismo a su 'Melodía Instantánea' y le dará más interés a su interpretación.
4. Toque las notas al mismo ritmo que le marque la canción.
5. Probablemente encontrará que, según en qué momento, ciertas notas son más adecuadas al acompañamiento que otras. Si toca una nota que no suena bien en un momento dado, simplemente vaya a la Nota de Solo más cercana, hacia arriba o hacia abajo.

La pista adicional "Jam" incluída en el disco, se ha compuesto especialmente para permitirle crear su propia melodía tocando cualquiera de las teclas negras, de una en una, en cualquier orden, junto con el acompañamiento. Si desea escuchar el tipo de melodías que se pueden crear utilizando las teclas negras, cargue la pista "Demo Jam" para oír los ejemplos de improvisaciones.

Cotenido Del Disco

1.	Yesterday	5.	Lady Madonna
2.	With A Little Help From My Friends	6.	Hey Jude
3.	Eleanor Rigby	7.	Penny Lane
4.	Michelle	8.	Let It Be

Para el procedimiento de cargar y reproducir los archivos mencionados arriba, remitase al manual del usuario de su reproductor se Standard MIDI Files.

Spielhinweise

Diesem Notenbuch ist eine völlig neue Art von Musikdaten-Diskette beigelegt. Diese 3.5" Diskette enthält digital aufgezeichnete Standard MIDI Files (SMF), die dem General MIDI (GM)-System entsprechen. Diese Files oder Musiktitel können auf jedem Sequenzer, der in der Lage ist, SMF-Daten zu lesen, abgespielt werden.

Die einzelnen Musiktitel enthalten zu der Melodie eine professionell arrangierte Begleitung. Sie können sich diese Musiktitel anhören oder selbst zu der Begleitung spielen.

Um die Melodie eines dieser Titel zu spielen (und anhand der 'Solo Noten' zu improvisieren), brauchen Sie nur den MIDI-Kanal oder die Spur, auf der sich die Daten für die Melodie befinden, stumm zu schalten. Bitte beachten Sie dazu die Bedienhinweise zu Ihrem Sequenzer und schalten Sie den MIDI-Kanal 4 oder die entsprechende Spur stumm.

Nun können Sie die Melodie selbst zur Begleitung spielen. Wenn Sie die 'Solo Noten' beachten, die im Abschnitt 'Spielhinweise' aufgeführt sind, ist es für Sie sehr einfach, zu der Begleitung zu improvisieren.

Die Musiktitel in diesem Buch sind so arrangiert, daß es für Sie sehr leicht ist, einfach mitzuspielen.

Die Begleit-Sektion einiger Keyboards ist unter Umständen nicht in der Lage, einige komplexe Akkorde innerhalb eines Musikstückes zu erkennen. Diese besonderen Akkorde sind grau gedruckt und können ignoriert werden, falls Ihr Keyboard diese Akkorde nicht erkennen kann oder Sie diese Akkorde noch nicht greifen können. Wenn Sie natürlich nach einiger Zeit diese komplexen Akkorde spielen können, klingt die Musik harmonisch viel interessanter.

Solo Noten

Immer, wenn Sie das logo 'Solo Noten' sehen, können Sie sehr leicht eine eigene Melodie improvisieren. Das oben abgebildete Logo hat als Beispiel Punkte auf den Tasten C, D, E, G und A. Mit diesen Noten können Sie zur Begleitung eine eigene, einstimmige Melodie improvisieren, egal in welcher Reihenfolge Sie diese Noten spielen (Music Minus One). Die 'Solo Noten' können in all den Takten gespielt werden, die durch eine graue Linie markiert sind. Die Anzahl dieser Takte ist innerhalb der einzelnen Musiktitel unterschiedlich.

Improvisations-Hinweise

1. Beginnen Sie, in dem Sie Ihre Finger auf die entsprechenden Tasten Ihres Instrumentes legen, die durch die Punkte gekennzeichnet sind. Spielen Sie eine mittlere Note dieser markierten 'Solo Noten' in einer beliebigen Oktave innerhalb der Melodie-(Upper-) Sektion Ihres Instrumentes.
2. Überlegen Sie, ob Sie Ihre gerade begonnene Melodie aufwärts oder abwärts (rechts oder links) weiterführen möchten.
3. Spielen Sie jetzt die nächst höhere oder tiefere Note nach Ihrer zuletzt gespielten Note. Wählen Sie gelegentlich einen 'größeren Schritt' (Intervall), indem Sie ein oder zwei 'Solo Noten' überspringen. Dadurch klingt Ihre selbst komponierte Melodie natürlicher und abwechslungsreicher.
4. Orientieren Sie sich am Metronom oder am Rhythmus der Musik.
5. Sie werden sicher feststellen, daß es Noten gibt, die an bestimmten Stellen des Musikstücks besser zur Begleitung passen als andere. Falls Sie eine Note spielen, die gerade nicht so gut zur Begleitung klingt, dann spielen Sie einfach die nächst höhere oder tiefere Note.

Die auf der Diskette zusätzlich enthaltene 'Jam'-Spur ist speziell dafür erstellt worden, damit Sie Ihre eigenen einstimmigen Melodien auf den schwarzen Tasten zur Begleitung spielen können.

Wenn Sie sich einige Beispiele anhören möchten, wie Melodien auf den schwarzen Tasten gespielt werden können, dann laden Sie die 'Demo Jam'-Spur mit den Improvisationsbeispielen und spielen Sie diese ab.

Inhalt der Diskette

1.	Yesterday	5.	Lady Madonna
2.	With A Little Help From My Friends	6.	Hey Jude
3.	Eleanor Rigby	7.	Penny Lane
4.	Michelle	8.	Let It Be

Bitte beachten Sie die Bedienungsanleitung Ihres Sequenzers bezüglich der Bedienschritte zum Laden und Abspielen der oben aufgeführten Files.

Suggerimenti sull'esecuzione

Allegato a questo libro, troverete un dischetto contenente nuovi dati musicali: su questo dischetto, di formato 3.5", sono registrati digitalmente brani in Standard MIDI File (SMF) che possono essere utilizzati su qualsiasi Computer possedente un riproduttore conforme al sistema General MIDI ed allo Standard MIDI File.

Il dischetto contiene la registrazione professionale di accompagnamenti e melodie per ogni brano inserito, su cui potrete suonare o semplicemente ascoltare; per poter suonare la melodia riguardante ogni brano (ed improvvisare utilizzando la funzione "Solo Notes"), dovete silenziare il canale MIDI (traccia) sul quale il dato è registrato. Seguendo le istruzioni proprie del vostro riproduttore, silenziate il canale MIDI 4 oppure la traccia sulla quale è posizionato il canale.

Suoniamo ora la melodia assieme all'accompagnamento: per improvvisare facilmente sull'accompagnamento, fate riferimento alla funzione "Solo Notes" (note di assolo) nel·seguente paragrafo "Suggerimenti sull'esecuzione".

I brani contenuti in questo testo sono stati particolarmente arrangiati al fine di semplificare l'esecuzione della melodia in base all'accompagnamento: in questa sezione possono però non essere riconosciuti alcuni degli Special Chords (accordi complessi), in dipendenza della tastiera elettronica utilizzata. Questi accordi complessi sono stampati in colore grigio, e possono essere ignorati nel caso la vostra tastiera non sia in grado di riconoscerli, oppure nel caso che vi siano ancora sconosciuti; naturalmente, quando a suo tempo avrete raggiunto la capacità di eseguire tutti gli accordi complessi, udirete un'armonizzazione molto migliorata.

Funzione Solo Notes (note di assolo)

Ogni qual volta vedrete la dicitura "Solo Notes" (note di assolo), potrete facilmente improvvisare la vostra melodia personalizzata: in questo caso, sulle seguenti note Do, Re, Mi, Sol e La appariranno dei puntini che indicano le note eseguibili. Potrete seguire, per queste note, un ordine di esecuzione casuale assieme alla traccia guida (metodo Music Minus One). Le note di assolo possono essere da voi suonate in corrispondenza di qualsiasi misura sulla quale sia visualizzata la linea grigia, che può variare in lunghezza da brano a brano.

Suggerimenti sull'improvvisazione

1. Iniziate posizionando le dita sulle note indicate dai puntini. Iniziate a suonare, in qualsiasi sezione della tastiera dedicata alla melodia (upper), una delle note "Solo" stabilite: tutto ciò in qualsiasi ottava dello strumento.
2. Decidete se la vostra improvvisazione sia ascendente o discendente (verso destra o verso sinistra).
3. Utilizzate quindi le note "Solo" più vicine a quella che state suonando (verso l'acuto o veso il grave). Fate occasionalmente trascorrere più tempo fra la pressione di due tasti. Questo aggiungerà maggiore realismo alla vostra improvvisazione e vi offrirà un maggiore divertimento.
4. Suonate seguendo il ritmo del brano.
5. Potete trovare note più indicate di altre riguardanti l'accompagnamento: suonando note che non "suonano bene" con esso, spostatevi semplicemente alla più vicina nota "Solo" verso l'acuto o verso il grave.

Su dischetto è inserita un'ulteriore traccia denominata "Jam", che vi consente di creare una melodia personalizzata utilizzando uno per volta i tasti neri in qualsiasi ordine; per rendervi conto delle melodie che possono essere create mediante questa traccia ed i tasti neri, provate a caricare e riprodurre la traccia "Demo Jam", contenente esempi di improvvisazione.

Contenuto del dischetto

1.	Yesterday	5.	Lady Madonna
2.	With A Little Help From My Friends	6.	Hey Jude
3.	Eleanor Rigby	7.	Penny Lane
4.	Michelle	8.	Let It Be

Fate riferimento al manuale d'uso del vostro riproduttore Standard MIDI File per tutte le procedure di caricamento e riproduzione dei suddetti brani.

Yesterday

Words and Music by John Lennon and Paul McCartney

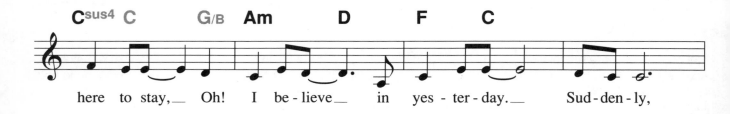

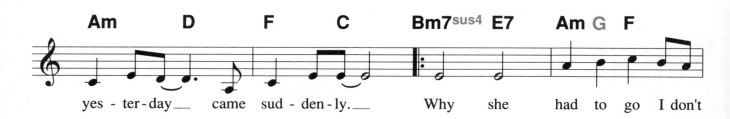

know   she would - n't say.____   I   said   some - thing wrong, now I

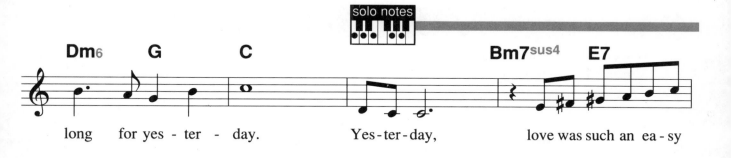

long   for yes - ter - day.   Yes - ter - day,   love was such an ea - sy

game   to play,____   Now I need a place to   hide   a - way,   Oh!

I   be - lieve   in   yes - ter - day. __   Mm mm mm mm   mm._____

With A Little Help From My Friends

Words and Music by John Lennon and Paul McCartney

What would you do __ if I sang __ out of tune __ would you stand __ up and walk __ out on me? __
(Verses 2&3 see block lyrics)

__ Lend me your ears __ and I'll sing __ you a song __ and I'll try __ not to sing __ out of key. __

__ Oh! I get by __ with a lit-tle help __ from my friends, __ mm, I get high __

__ with a lit-tle help __ from my friends, __ mm, I'm gon-na try __

__ with a lit-tle help __ from my friends. __

2. What do I do when my love is away,
   Is it worrying to be alone?
   How do I feel by the end of the day?
   Are you sad because you're on your own?
   No, I get by with a little help from my friends,
   Mm, I get high with a little help from my friends,
   Mm, I'm gonna try with a little help from my friends.

3. Would you believe in a love at first sight?
   Yes, I'm certain that it happens all the time.
   What do you see when you turn out the light?
   I can't tell you but I know it's mine.
   Oh, I get by with a little help from my friends,
   Mm, I get high with a little help from my friends,
   Mm, I'm gonna try with a little help from my friends.

Eleanor Rigby

Words and Music by John Lennon and Paul McCartney

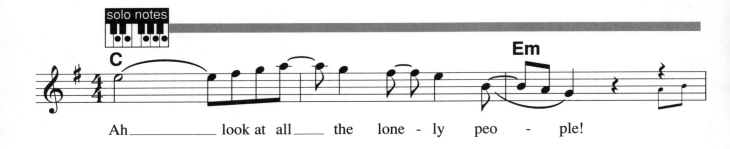

Ah_____ look at all___ the lone - ly peo - - ple!

Ah_____ look at all___ the lone - ly peo - - ple!

1. E - lea - nor Rig - by, picks up the rice___ in the church.
(Verses 2&3 see block lyrics)

___ where a wed - ding has been,___ lives in a dream . ___ Waits at the win - dow,

wear-ing the face___ that she keeps___ in a jar___ by the door,___

Who is it for?___ All the lone - ly peo - ple, where do___

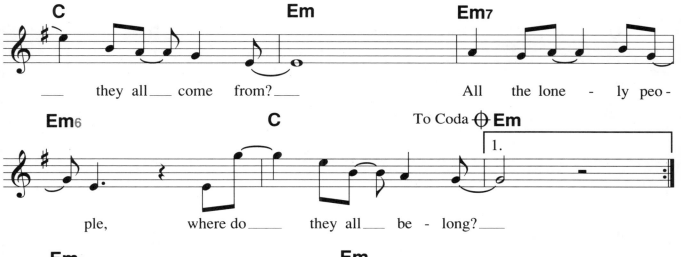

___ they all___ come from?___ All the lone - ly peo -

ple, where do___ they all___ be - long?___

2. D.C. al Coda

Coda

2. Father McKenzie,
   Writing the words of a sermon,
   That no-one will hear,
   No-one comes near.
   Look at him working,
   Darning his socks in the night
   When there's nobody there,
   What does he care?

3. Eleanor Rigby,
   Died in the church
   And was buried along with her name,
   Nobody came.
   Father McKenzie,
   Wiping the dirt from his hands
   As he walks from the grave,
   No-one was saved.

   Repeat Chorus

Michelle

Words and Music by John Lennon and Paul McCartney

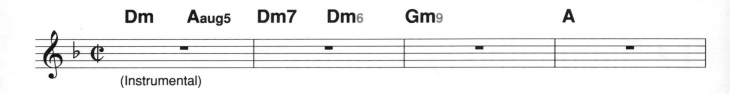

(Instrumental)

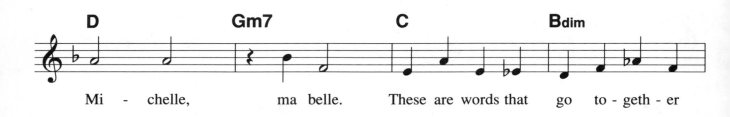

Mi - chelle, ma belle. These are words that go to - geth - er

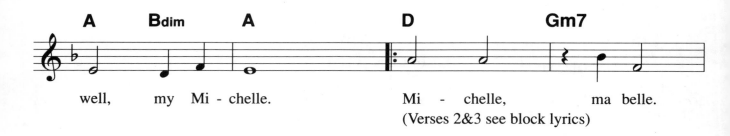

well, my Mi - chelle. Mi - chelle, ma belle.
(Verses 2&3 see block lyrics)

Sont les mots qui vont très bien en - semble, très bien en - semble. I

love you, I love you, I love you,   That's all I want to

say.   Un-til I find a way, _____ I will

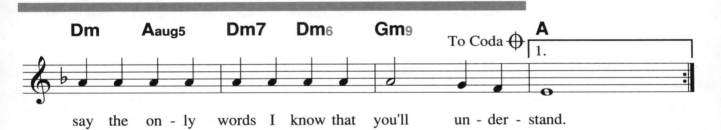

say the on-ly words I know that you'll un-der-stand.

mean.   (Guitar Instrumental)

I

15

stand. Mi - chelle, ma belle

Sont les mots qui vont très bien en - semble, très bien en - semble. I will

say the on - ly words I know that you'll un - der - stand, my Mi -

chelle. (Guitar Instrumental)

Repeat and fade

2. Michelle, ma belle.
   Sont les mots qui vont très bien ensemble,
   Très bien ensemble.
   I need to, I need to, I need to.
   I need to make you see
   What you mean to me.
   Until I do,
   I'm hoping you will know what I mean.
   I love you.

3. I want you, I want you, I want you.
   I think you know by now.
   I'll get to you somehow.
   Until I do,
   I'm telling you so you'll understand.

   Michelle, ma belle.
   Sont les mots qui vont très bien ensemble,
   Très bien ensemble.
   I will say the only words
   I know that you'll understand, my Michelle.

16

Lady Madonna

Words and Music by John Lennon and Paul McCartney

Introduction (Instrumental)

La-dy Ma-don-na chil-dren at your feet, Won-der how you ma-nage to make __ ends meet. __ Who finds the mo-ney when you pay the rent, __

Did you think that mo-ney was __ Hea-ven sent. __ Fri-day night __ ar-rives with-out a
(See block lyric)

See how they run. La-dy Ma-don-na Ba-by at your breast,

Won-der how you ma-nage to feed___ the rest.___ (Instrumental)

D.S. al Coda

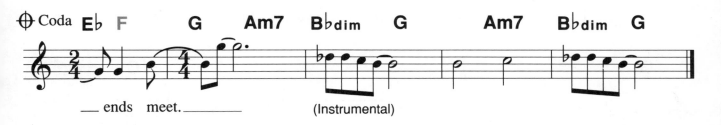

___ ends meet._____ (Instrumental)

Lady Madonna, lying on the bed,
Listen to the music playing in your head.

Tuesday afternoon is never ending,
Wednesday morning papers didn't come.
Thursday night your stockings needed mending,
See how they'll run.

Lady Madonna, children at your feet,
Wonder how you manage to make ends meet.

Hey Jude

Words and Music by John Lennon and Paul McCartney

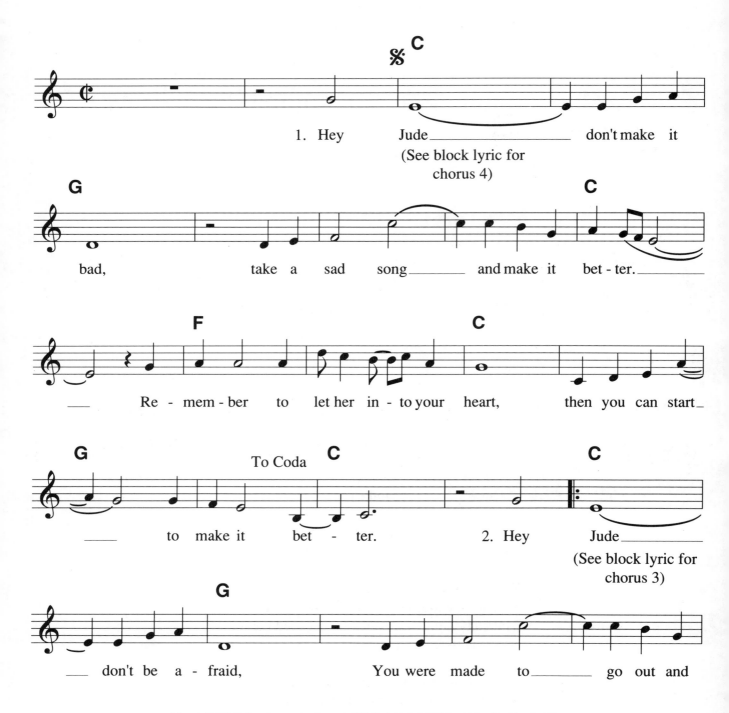

1. Hey Jude_____ don't make it
(See block lyric for chorus 4)

bad, take a sad song_____ and make it bet - ter._____

___ Re - mem - ber to let her in - to your heart, then you can start_

To Coda

___ to make it bet - ter. 2. Hey Jude_____
(See block lyric for chorus 3)

___ don't be a - fraid, You were made to_____ go out and

get her.____ The min - ute you let her un - der your

skin, then you be - gin_____ to make it bet -

ter. And a - ny time___ you feel the

pain, Hey Jude_____ re - frain.____ Don't car - ry the world__

___ u - pon_____ your shoul - ders._____

For now you know that it's a fool who plays____ it cool__

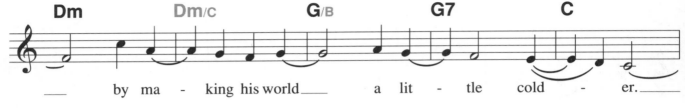

by ma - king his world___ a lit - tle cold - er.___

Da Da Da Da Da Da Da Da Da

1. Hey

2. Hey

D.S. al Coda

Coda **C**

- ter, bet - ter, bet - ter, bet - ter,

solo notes

bet - ter, bet - ter, Oh! Da, da, da, da, da, da, da,___

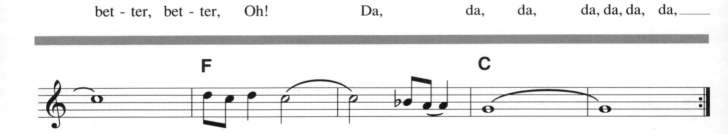

___ da, da, da, da,_____ Hey ___ Jude._____

3. Hey Jude, don't let me down,
   You have found her, now go and get her,
   Remember to let her into your heart,
   Then you can start to make it better.
   So let it out and let it in.
   Hey Jude, begin,
   You're waiting for someone to perform with.
   And don't you know that it's just you.
   Hey Jude, you'll do.
   The movement you need is on your shoulder.
   Da, da, da, da, da, da, da, da, da, da.

4. Hey Jude, don't make it bad;
   Take a sad song and make it better.
   Remember to let her under your skin,
   Then you'll begin to make it
   Better, better, better, better, better, better.
   Yeah.

Penny Lane

Words and Music by John Lennon and Paul McCartney

In Pen-ny Lane ___ there is a bar-ber show-ing pho-to-graphs ___ of ev-'ry head
(See block lyric)

___ he's had the plea-sure to ___ know. And all the peo-ple that come and go ___

___ stop and say ___ "hel-lo". On the cor-ner there's a ban-ker with a

mo-tor car, ___ the lit-tle chil-dren laugh at him be-hind his back. And the

ban-ker ne-ver wears a mac ___ in the pour - ing rain.

Pen-ny Lane___ is in my ears___ and in my eyes.___

___ A four of fish___ and fin-ger pies___ in sum-mer mean-while___back, be-hind the

mean - while ___ back, Pen-ny Lane___ is in my ears___ and in my eyes.___

There be-neath the blue___ su-bur-ban skies,___

Pen-ny Lane._____

Meanwhile, back behind the shelter
In the middle of the roundabout,
A pretty nurse is selling poppies from a tray.
And tho' she feels as if she's in a play, she is anyway.

In Penny Lane the barber shaves another customer
We see the banker sitting waiting for a trim,
And the fireman rushes in from the pouring rain.
Very strange.

Let It Be

Words and Music by John Lennon and Paul McCartney

Introduction

(1.) When I find my-self in times of trou-ble, Mo-ther Ma-ry
(Verses 2&3 see block lyrics)

comes to me Speak-ing words of wis - dom, let it be.___

And in my hour of dark - ness, She is stan-ding right in front

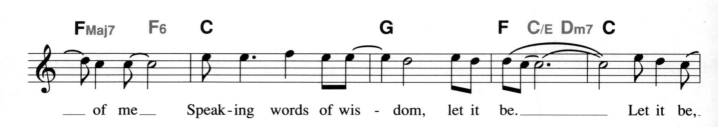

__ of me___ Speak-ing words of wis - dom, let it be._____ Let it be,

let it be,_____ let it be,_____ let it be,_____

Whis-per words__ of wis - dom,__ let it be._____ And

_____ Let it be,___ let it be,_

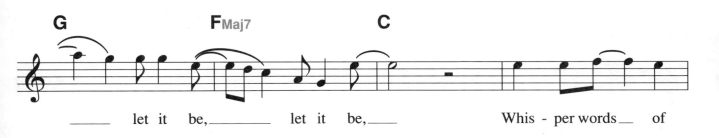

_____ let it be,_____ let it be,___ Whis - per words__ of

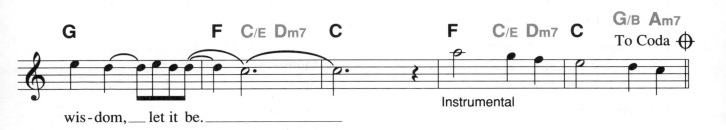

wis - dom,__ let it be._____ Instrumental

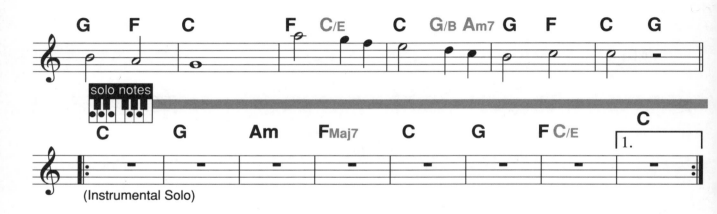

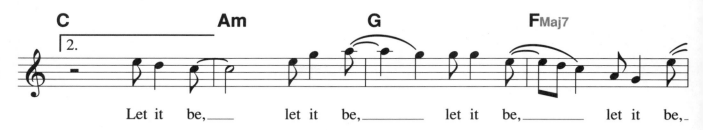

(Instrumental Solo)

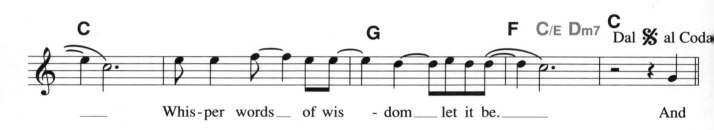

Let it be,____ let it be,_____ let it be,_____ let it be,_

____ Whis-per words__ of wis - dom__ let it be._____ And

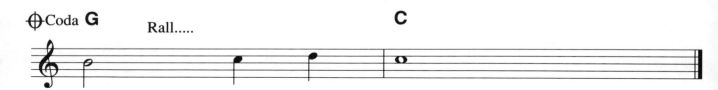

2. And when the broken hearted people,
   Living in the world agree,
   There will be an answer, let it be.

   For though they may be parted,
   There is still a chance that they will see
   There will be an answer, let it be.

   Let it be, let it be,
   Let it be, let it be,
   There will be an answer, let it be.

3. And when the night is cloudy,
   There is still a light that shines on me,
   Shine until tomorrow, let it be.

   I wake up to the sound of music,
   Mother Mary comes to me,
   Speaking words of wisdom, let it be.

   Let it be, let it be,
   Let it be, let it be,
   There will be an answer, let it be.
   Let it be, let it be,
   Let it be, let it be,
   Whisper words of wisdom, let it be.